GW01339082

COUNTRY PROFILES
ARGENTINA

BY CHRISTINA LEAF

BELLWETHER MEDIA • MINNEAPOLIS, MN

Blastoff! Discovery launches a new mission: reading to learn. Filled with facts and features, each book offers you an exciting new world to explore!

This edition first published in 2020 by Bellwether Media, Inc.

No part of this publication may be reproduced in whole or in part without written permission of the publisher.
For information regarding permission, write to Bellwether Media, Inc., Attention: Permissions Department, 6012 Blue Circle Drive, Minnetonka, MN 55343.

Library of Congress Cataloging-in-Publication Data

Names: Leaf, Christina, author.
Title: Argentina / by Christina Leaf.
Description: Minneapolis, MN : Bellwether Media, Inc., 2020. |
 Series: Blastoff! Discovery: Country Profiles | Includes bibliographical
  references and index. | Audience: Ages 7-13.
Identifiers: LCCN 2019001492 (print) | LCCN 2019002727 (ebook)
  | ISBN 9781618915870 (ebook) | ISBN 9781644870464
  (hardcover : alk. paper)
Subjects: LCSH: Argentina–Juvenile literature.
Classification: LCC F2808.2 (ebook) | LCC F2808.2 .L43 2020
  (print) | DDC 982–dc23
LC record available at https://lccn.loc.gov/2019001492

Text copyright © 2020 by Bellwether Media, Inc. BLASTOFF! DISCOVERY and associated logos are trademarks and/or registered trademarks of Bellwether Media, Inc. SCHOLASTIC, CHILDREN'S PRESS, and associated logos are trademarks and/or registered trademarks of Scholastic Inc., 557 Broadway, New York, NY 10012.

Editor: Rebecca Sabelko   Designer: Brittany McIntosh

Printed in the United States of America, North Mankato, MN.

TABLE OF CONTENTS

THE PASSION OF THE CITY	4
LOCATION	6
LANDSCAPE AND CLIMATE	8
WILDLIFE	10
PEOPLE	12
COMMUNITIES	14
CUSTOMS	16
SCHOOL AND WORK	18
PLAY	20
FOOD	22
CELEBRATIONS	24
TIMELINE	26
ARGENTINA FACTS	28
GLOSSARY	30
TO LEARN MORE	31
INDEX	32

THE PASSION OF THE CITY

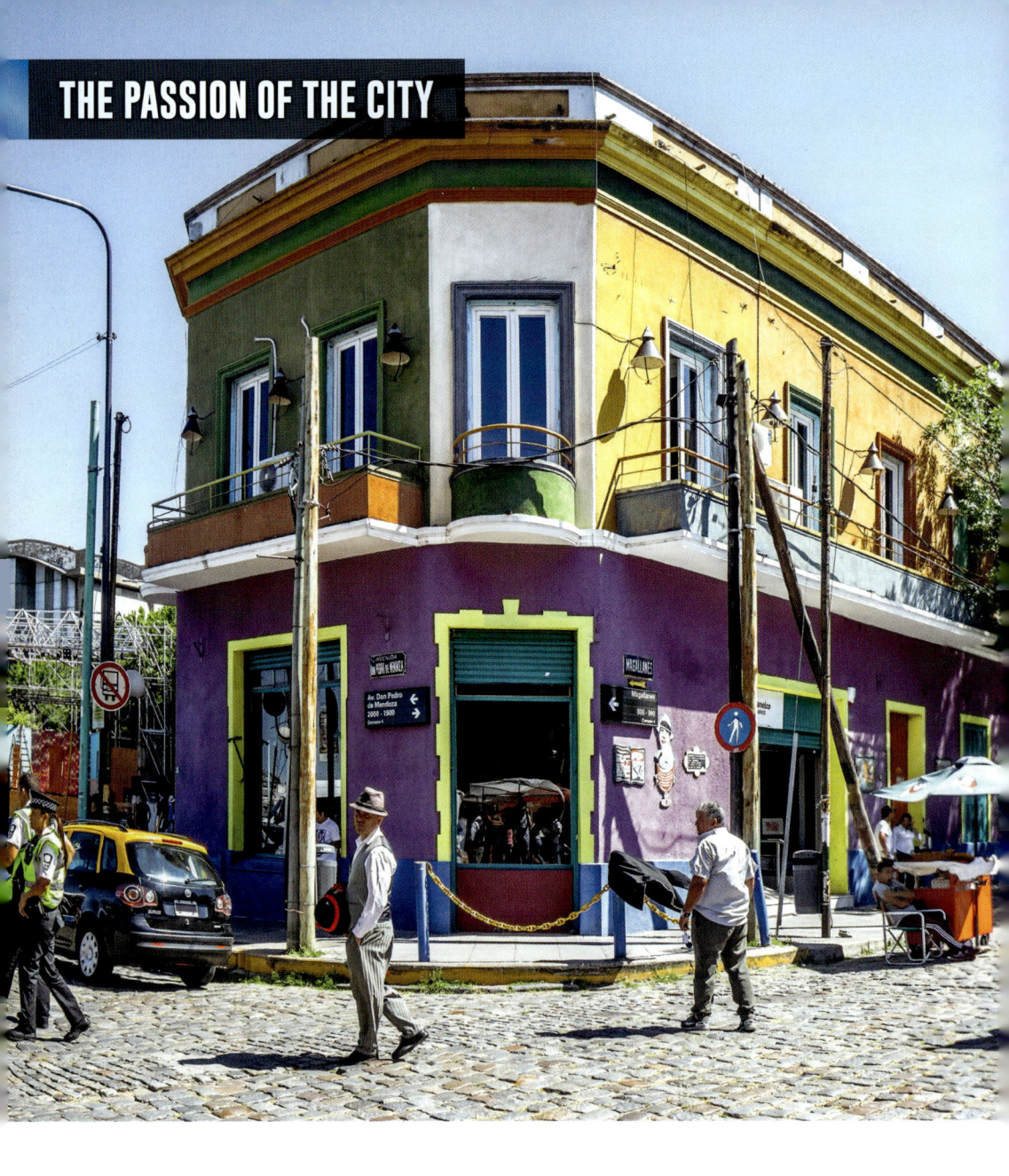

   Soft tango melodies fill the air as a family walks through the Buenos Aires neighborhood of La Boca. Around them, brightly colored apartment buildings reach toward the sky. Artists and dancers show off their talent for crowds on the street.

LA BOCA
BUENOS AIRES

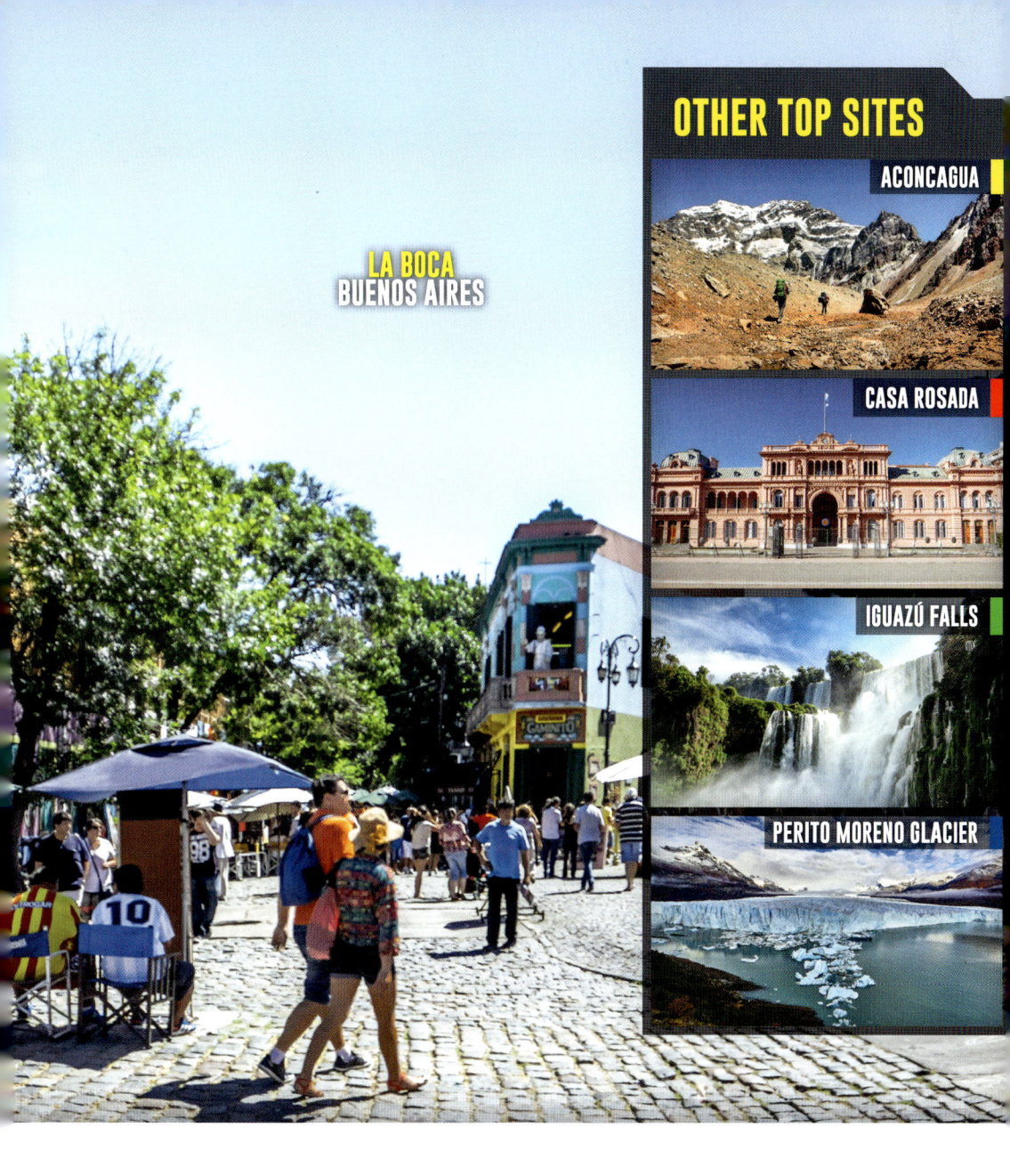

OTHER TOP SITES

ACONCAGUA

CASA ROSADA

IGUAZÚ FALLS

PERITO MORENO GLACIER

The family stops for a lunch of piping hot *empanadas*. Then they head to La Bombonera to take in a soccer game. Passionate fans all around the family cheer on Boca Juniors as the players take shots and make saves. The music, color, and passion are just a small part of what Argentina has to offer!

LOCATION

BOLIVIA
PARAGUAY
CÓRDOBA
ROSARIO
MENDOZA
BUENOS AIRES
BRAZIL
URUGUAY
CHILE
ARGENTINA
ATLANTIC OCEAN
STRAIT OF MAGELLAN
TIERRA DEL FUEGO

6

Argentina covers most of the southern part of South America. This long, narrow country stretches across 1,073,518 square miles (2,780,400 square kilometers). The capital, Buenos Aires, lies on the country's northeastern coast.

The Atlantic Ocean washes along Argentina's eastern border. Uruguay and Brazil also lie to the east. To the north sit Paraguay and Bolivia. Chile is across the Andes Mountains on Argentina's western edge. The very southern tip of Argentina is called *Tierra del Fuego*, or "land of fire." The **Strait** of Magellan separates it from the rest of the country.

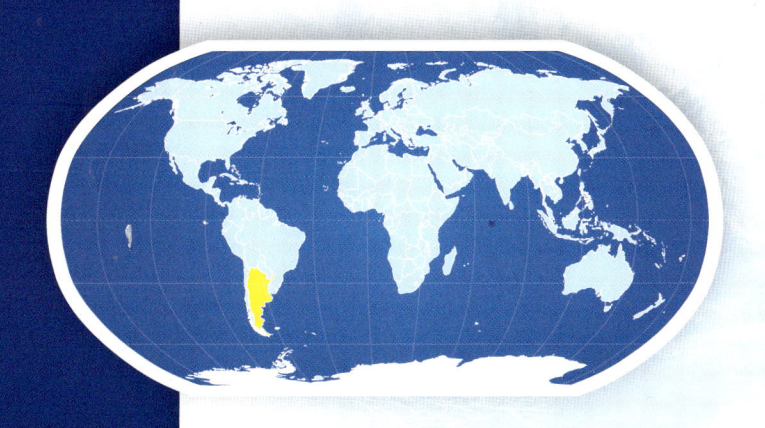

LANDSCAPE AND CLIMATE

Argentina has four main landscapes. In the north, the **terrain** is covered by dry **scrubland**. The scrub becomes **fertile** lowlands in the northeast. Cutting through the north flows the Paraná River. It empties into the Atlantic in the east. The rolling grasslands of Las Pampas fill central Argentina.

PARANÁ RIVER

= ANDES MOUNTAINS
= LAS PAMPAS
= PATAGONIA

PASO DE JAMA
ANDES MOUNTAINS

IGUAZÚ FALLS

BUENOS AIRES

Average seasonal highs and lows

JANUARY
HIGH: 84 °F (29 °C)
LOW: 63 °F (17 °C)

APRIL
HIGH: 72 °F (22 °C)
LOW: 54 °F (12 °C)

JULY
HIGH: 57 °F (14 °C)
LOW: 43 °F (6 °C)

OCTOBER
HIGH: 70 °F (21 °C)
LOW: 50 °F (10 °C)

°F = degrees Fahrenheit
°C = degrees Celsius

A LOT OF WATER
Iguazú Falls is on the border of Argentina and Brazil. It is made up of 275 small waterfalls!

   The tall mountains of the Andes tower over western Argentina. In the south, the dry, rocky terrain of Patagonia covers the country's tip.
   Argentina's climate is mostly **temperate**. Winters are mild in the north, while summers can be hot. Rain falls mostly in the northeast.

WILDLIFE

Argentina's huge size and varied landscape means it hosts a wide variety of animals. Guanacos roam the slopes of the Andes. In the forests of the north, jaguars and ocelots hunt animals such as capybaras and fish.

Few **native** animals still wander the Pampas. Flightless greater rheas share the land with deer and small mammals such as hares and plains viscachas. The rocky shores of Patagonia are home to sea lions and Magellanic penguins. Whales swim off the southern coasts.

CAPYBARA

OCELOT

GREATER RHEA

PLAINS VISCACHA

MAGELLANIC PENGUINS

GUANACO

GUANACO

Life Span: up to 28 years
Red List Status: least concern

guanaco range =

| LEAST CONCERN | NEAR THREATENED | VULNERABLE | ENDANGERED | CRITICALLY ENDANGERED | EXTINCT IN THE WILD | EXTINCT |

11

PEOPLE

Heavy **immigration** starting in the late 1800s means that most of Argentina's nearly 45 million people have European backgrounds. Spanish and Italian are the most common. A small population is *mestizo*, with native and European backgrounds. The few native Argentinians live in **remote** areas.

12

Spanish is the official language of Argentina, but many people speak Italian or English as well. The Roman Catholic religion is a big part of Argentina's **culture**. Most people identify with the religion, even if many do not attend church regularly. Argentina has small Jewish and Protestant communities, too.

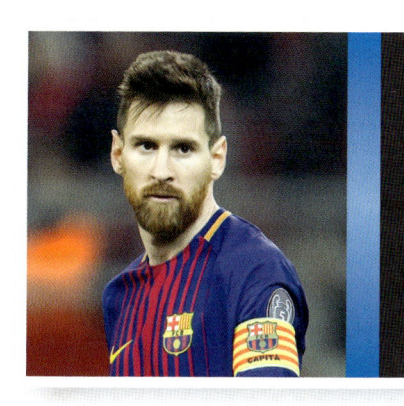

FAMOUS FACE

Name: Lionel Messi
Birthday: June 24, 1987
Hometown: Rosario, Argentina
Famous for: A star forward for the FC Barcelona soccer team who has also led the Argentina national team in four World Cups

SPEAK SPANISH

ENGLISH	SPANISH	HOW TO SAY IT
hello	hola	OH-lah
goodbye	adiós	ah-dee-OHS
please	por favor	pohr fah-VOR
thank you	gracias	grah-SEE-ahs
yes	sí	SEE
no	no	noh

BUENOS AIRES

COMMUNITIES

Argentinians mostly live in cities. Many rent apartments in tall buildings in the heart of the city. Lower-income families crowd together in small shacks. **Rural** Argentinians mostly live in single-family homes. Styles vary by area, with **adobe** houses common in the south and whitewashed houses popular in the hot north. Wealthy ranch owners may live in large houses called *estancias*.

QUITE A STREET
One of the widest streets in the world is in Buenos Aires. The 9 de Julio Avenue is as wide as a city block!

Railways connect most of Argentina's cities. Cars are common, but in cities, people generally use subways and buses to get around.

15

CUSTOMS

Food and drink are at the center of Argentina's customs. Across the country, people share the **ritual** of drinking hot *mate* made from the *yerba mate* plant. This earthy tea is sipped out of a gourd through a metal straw. Friends pass the gourd around, sharing and refilling with hot water when needed.

On weekends, people gather for *asados*, which are similar to barbeques. At these, meat is specially cooked over a wood fire while everyone spends time with friends and family. Argentinians take an unhurried attitude toward asados. The events can take up half a day!

RIGHT ON TIME
Guests are not expected to arrive on time in Argentina. Arriving up to 60 minutes after the agreed upon time is acceptable.

SCHOOL AND WORK

Most Argentinian children attend public schools. Children must have two years of preschool. Then they attend school for 12 years, beginning at age 6. Primary school lasts for 6 or 7 years. Secondary school begins with general education. Students can study specific topics later in secondary school.

Argentina is known for its rich **natural resources**. Miners dig up **petroleum** and precious metals such as silver and gold. Workers turn these resources into goods including cars and other machinery. Farmers raise cattle and wheat on the wide plains of the Pampas. **Tourism** and other **service industries** employ most Argentinians.

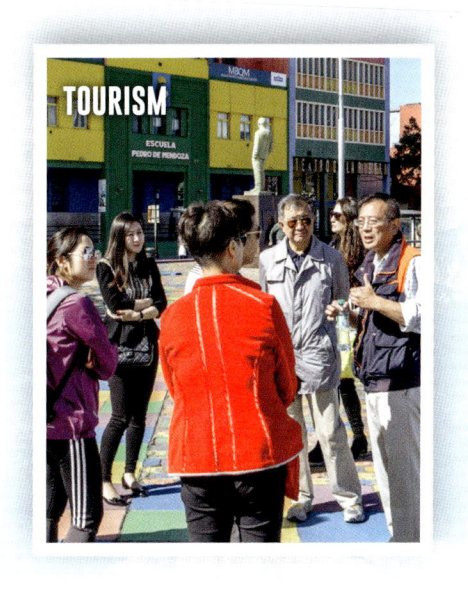

TOURISM

COWBOY LIFE

Some Argentinians still work as cowboys, called *gauchos*. Their history and work continue to play a large part in Argentina's cultural identity.

GAUCHOS

PLAY

TANGO

Tango began in Argentina in the late nineteenth century. Older generations treasure listening to and dancing tango. However, younger people are more likely to listen to modern music.

Soccer is the favorite sport in Argentina. Fans cheer on the national team or local clubs with great enthusiasm. Argentina's national sport is *pato*. This game began among gauchos on the Pampas. In it, players on horseback pass a ball with six handles back and forth and try to get it into a hoop. Polo, basketball, and rugby are other popular sports.

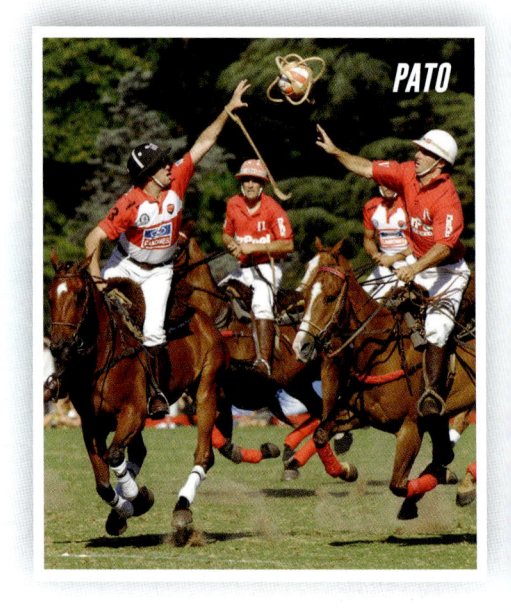

PATO

20

In winter, the southern Andes draw skiers to their slopes. Hiking is popular in Patagonia in the summer. Singing and dancing are common across the country in all seasons. Kids also like to watch television and play video games.

HIKING

¡ALTO AHÍ! (STOP THERE!)

What You Need:
- 3 or more players
- a ball
- an open space

Instructions:
1. One player takes the ball, and the other players begin running.
2. The player with the ball calls "Stop there!" and names a player.
3. The player with the ball gets three steps toward the named player. Then they throw the ball toward the player.
4. If the ball touches the named player, that player has a "spot" and becomes the player with the ball. If the ball misses, the named player is "clean" and the first player has to name a different player to throw the ball to.
5. The first player with three spots has to do something silly or embarrassing, decided on by the group. If they do it, the game continues. If they refuse, they have to do two silly things. Then the game starts over and everyone is "clean."

FOOD

MORE MEAT
Llama is often eaten in the northwest of Argentina. The animals are common around the Andes.

PARRILLA

Argentinians eat more beef than nearly anyone else in the world. Families like to cook it on the *parrilla*, or grill. Cities are filled with steakhouses, also called parrillas. Pasta and pizza are common, thanks to Argentina's Italian population.

For light meals, Argentinians might snack on savory pastries called empanadas. Hot sandwiches including *choripán* and breaded *milanesas* are also popular. Sweet pastries called *medialunas* might be found at breakfast or with afternoon tea. *Alfajores* are a treat for dessert. These sandwich cookies are often filled with the caramel-like *dulce de leche*.

EMPANADAS

ALFAJORES

DULCE DE LECHE

Argentinians love this sweet sauce! Have an adult help you make this recipe.

Ingredients:
1 14-ounce can of sweetened condensed milk

Steps:
1. Preheat the oven to 425 degrees Fahrenheit (218 degrees Celsius), with the rack in the middle.
2. Pour the condensed milk into a pie plate, and cover it with foil.
3. Put the plate in a large, deep pan. Fill the pan with hot water until it reaches halfway up the side of the pie plate, and place them into the oven.
4. Bake for 45 minutes, then check the water. Add more if needed.
5. Bake for another 45 minutes until the milk is thick and brown. Remove the pie plate and the foil, and allow it to cool. Add to cookies or ice cream and enjoy!

CELEBRATIONS

Most Argentinians observe Christian holidays. On Easter, towns have processions and church services. After, families gather for asado and eat special braided bread. Since Argentina is in the southern **hemisphere**, Christmas falls in the summer. Cities light impressive fireworks displays at midnight on Christmas Eve. Afterwards, people go dancing until late in the night.

A NEW HOLIDAY

In October, Argentinians celebrate the Day of Respect for Cultural Diversity. This day used to be Columbus Day. The country changed it to honor the native peoples who were taken over by the Spanish.

CHRISTMAS

CARNAVAL

One of Argentina's biggest celebrations is *Carnaval* in February. People head to the town of Gualeguaychú for colorful festivities. Argentinians also celebrate the 1810 revolution each year on May 25. On this national holiday, marches, public speeches, and **traditional** foods help Argentinians show pride for their country!

TIMELINE

1580
Buenos Aires becomes a stable Spanish settlement

1812
José de San Martín leads a revolution against Spain

1816
Argentina declares independence from Spain

1861
The Argentine Confederation and the state of Buenos Aires join to become a united country

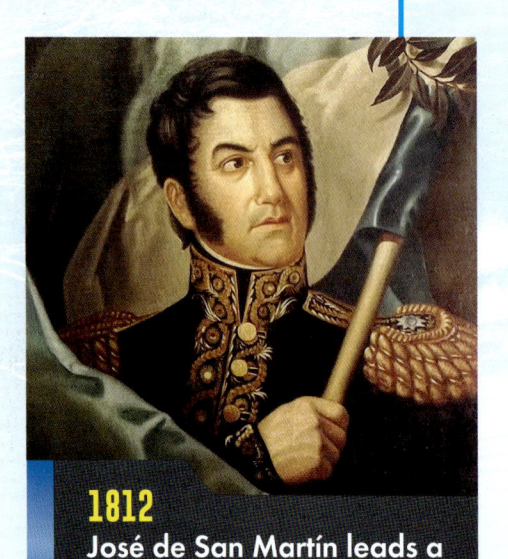

LATE 1800s – 1930s
Millions of Europeans immigrate to Argentina to find work and freedom

1976-1983
Thousands of people who oppose the government go missing in what becomes known as the Dirty War

1974
Juan Perón's third wife, Isabel, becomes the first female president in the world when Juan dies

1982
Argentina and Great Britain fight for control of the Falkland Islands

2010
Argentina is the first country in Latin America to make same-sex marriage legal

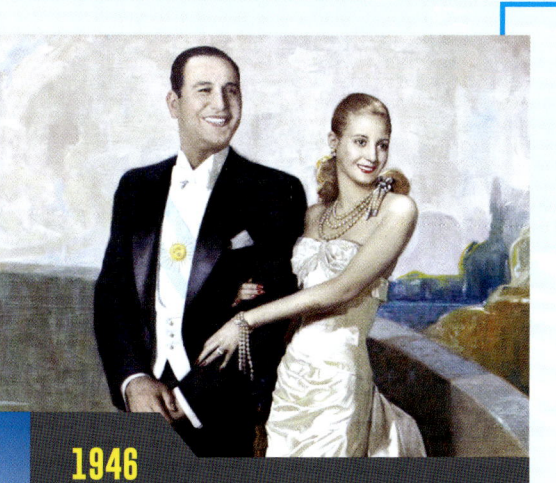

1946
Juan Perón is elected president, and he and his wife, Eva, gain huge popularity with Argentina's working class

ARGENTINA FACTS

Official Name: Argentine Republic

Flag of Argentina: Three horizontal bands, with a white band in the middle of two light blue bands. Some believe the colors represent the blue sky and clouds on the day Argentina gained control of its government from the Spanish. Others think it was because the patriots wore pale blue uniforms. In the middle of the flag, a golden sun represents the sun shining through the clouds on that day.

Area: 1,073,518 square miles (2,780,400 square kilometers)

Capital City: Buenos Aires

Important Cities: Córdoba, Rosario, Mendoza

Population: 44,694,198 (July 2018)

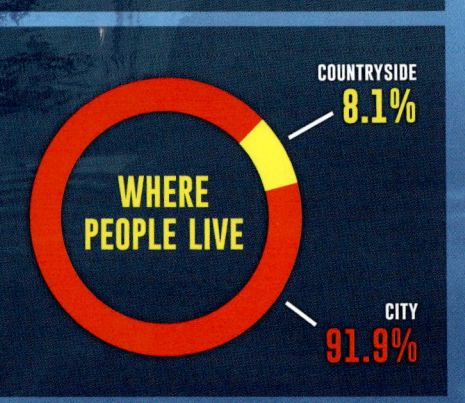

WHERE PEOPLE LIVE
- COUNTRYSIDE 8.1%
- CITY 91.9%

JOBS

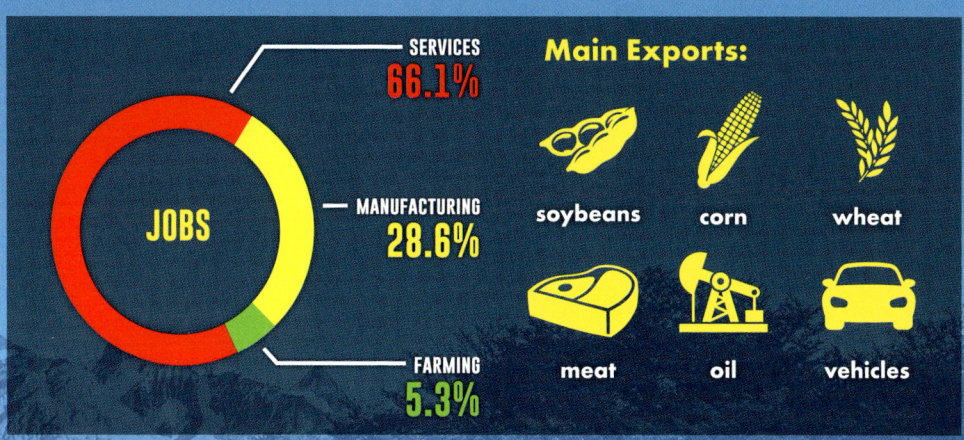

- SERVICES **66.1%**
- MANUFACTURING **28.6%**
- FARMING **5.3%**

Main Exports:

- soybeans
- corn
- wheat
- meat
- oil
- vehicles

National Holiday:
Revolution Day (May 25)

Main Language:
Spanish

Form of Government:
presidential republic

Title for Country Leader:
president

RELIGION

- PROTESTANT **2%**
- OTHER **4%**
- JEWISH **2%**
- ROMAN CATHOLIC **92%**

Unit of Money:
Argentine peso

29

GLOSSARY

adobe—related to bricks made of clay and straw that are dried in the sun

culture—the beliefs, arts, and ways of life in a place or society

fertile—able to support growth

hemisphere—a half of the earth

immigration—the act of moving from one country to another

native—originally from the area or related to a group of people or animals that began in the area

natural resources—materials in the earth that are taken out and used to make products or fuel

petroleum—an oily liquid found in the earth than can be used to make many products, including gasoline

remote—far removed

ritual—an act or series of acts that are regularly repeated in the same way

rural—related to the countryside

scrubland—dry land that has mostly low plants and few trees

service industries—groups of businesses that perform tasks for people or businesses

strait—a narrow channel connecting two large bodies of water

temperate—associated with a mild climate that does not have extreme heat or cold

terrain—the surface features of an area of land

tourism—the business of people traveling to visit other places

traditional—related to customs, ideas, or beliefs handed down from one generation to the next

TO LEARN MORE

AT THE LIBRARY

Fishman, Jon M. *Lionel Messi*. Minneapolis, Minn.: Lerner Publications, 2018.

Mattern, Joanne. *Argentina*. New York, N.Y.: Cavendish Square, 2019.

Morganelli, Adrianna. *Cultural Traditions in Argentina*. New York, N.Y.: Crabtree Publishing, 2016.

ON THE WEB

FACTSURFER

Factsurfer.com gives you a safe, fun way to find more information.

1. Go to www.factsurfer.com.

2. Enter "Argentina" into the search box and click 🔍.

3. Select your book cover to see a list of related web sites.

INDEX

1810 revolution, 25
activities, 20, 21
alto ahí (activity), 21
Buenos Aires, 4, 5, 6, 7, 9, 13, 15
capital (see Buenos Aires)
Carnaval, 25
celebrations, 24-25
Christmas, 24
climate, 9
communities, 14-15
customs, 16-17, 19, 22
Day of Respect for Cultural Diversity, 24
Easter, 24
education, 18
fast facts, 28-29
food, 5, 16, 17, 22-23, 24, 25
Gualeguaychú, 25
housing, 4, 14
La Boca, 4-5
landmarks, 5
landscape, 7, 8-9, 10, 19, 20, 21, 22
language, 13

location, 6-7, 24
Messi, Lionel, 13
people, 12-13, 22, 24
recipe, 23
religion, 13, 24
size, 7, 10
sports, 5, 20, 21
timeline, 26-27
transportation, 15
wildlife, 10-11
work, 19

The images in this book are reproduced through the courtesy of: dsaprin, cover; Diego Grandi, pp. 4-5, 9 (right), 13, 15; canadastock, p. 5 (top); saiko3p, p. 5 (top middle); sharptoyou, p. 5 (bottom middle); Ionov Vitaly, p. 5 (bottom); AridOcean, pp. 6-7, 8 (top); Ksenia Ragozina, p. 8; Det-anan, p. 9; Anan Kaewkhammul, p. 10 (left); Omariam, p. 10 (top); Pablo Rodriguez Merkel, p. 10 (middle top); Danita Delimont/ Alamy, p. 10 (middle bottom); Sergey Didenko, p. 10 (bottom); Palm Yutthana, pp. 10-11; Education & Exploration 1/ Alamy, p. 12; Ververidis Vasillis, p. 13 (top); reisegraf.ch, p. 14; imageBroker/ Alamy, p. 16; T photography, p. 17; Xinhua/ Alamy, p. 18; Jeff Greenberg/ Alamy, p. 19; sunsinger, p. 19; Bill BAchmann/ Alamy, p. 20 (top); buteo/ Alamy, p. 20; Galyna Andrushko, p. 21 (top); Konstantin Shishkin/ Alamy, p. 21; robertharding/ Alamy, p. 22; yasuhiro amano, p. 23 (top); AS Food studio, p. 23 (middle); Beto Chagas, p. 23 (bottom); Krzysztof Dydynski/ Getty, p. 24; Awakening/ Getty, p. 25; Offnfopt/ Wiki Commons, p. 26; CherylRamalho, p. 27 (top); World History Archive/ Alamy, p. 27 (bottom); Ivsanmas, p. 28; Anton_Ivanov, p. 29; Fat Jackey, p. 29 (coin).